Perfect daily Maths practice from CGP!

Year 1 is full of essential Maths skills that pupils need to learn. Thankfully, CGP's daily practice is here to make sure all that vital knowledge sinks in...

This book contains heaps of Maths activities, with one for every day of the summer term, covering a different skill from the Year 1 curriculum.

Plus, it's packed with engaging pictures to make sure pupils stay interested, and handy examples. It's ideal for in class, recaps, homework tasks... and more!

What CGP is all about

Our sole aim here at CGP is to produce the highest quality books — carefully written, immaculately presented and dangerously close to being funny.

Then we work our socks off to get them out to you — at the cheapest possible prices.

Contents

☑ Use the tick boxes to help keep a record of which tests have been attempted.

Week 1
☑ Day 1 1
☑ Day 2 2
☑ Day 3 3
☑ Day 4 4
☑ Day 5 5

Week 2
☑ Day 1 6
☑ Day 2 7
☑ Day 3 8
☑ Day 4 9
☑ Day 5 10

Week 3
☑ Day 1 11
☑ Day 2 12
☑ Day 3 13
☑ Day 4 14
☑ Day 5 15

Week 4
☑ Day 1 16
☑ Day 2 17
☑ Day 3 18
☑ Day 4 19
☑ Day 5 20

Week 5
☑ Day 1 21
☑ Day 2 22
☑ Day 3 23
☑ Day 4 24
☑ Day 5 25

Week 6
☑ Day 1 26
☑ Day 2 27
☑ Day 3 28
☑ Day 4 29
☑ Day 5 30

Week 7
☑ Day 1 31
☑ Day 2 32
☑ Day 3 33
☑ Day 4 34
☑ Day 5 35

Week 8
☑ Day 1 36
☑ Day 2 37
☑ Day 3 38
☑ Day 4 39
☑ Day 5 40

Week 9

- [✓] Day 1 41
- [✓] Day 2 42
- [✓] Day 3 43
- [✓] Day 4 44
- [✓] Day 5 45

Week 10

- [✓] Day 1 46
- [✓] Day 2 47
- [✓] Day 3 48
- [✓] Day 4 49
- [✓] Day 5 50

Week 11

- [✓] Day 1 51
- [✓] Day 2 52
- [✓] Day 3 53
- [✓] Day 4 54
- [✓] Day 5 55

Week 12

- [✓] Day 1 56
- [✓] Day 2 57
- [✓] Day 3 58
- [✓] Day 4 59
- [✓] Day 5 60

Published by CGP

ISBN: 978 1 78908 506 8

Editors: Eleanor Crabtree, Josie Gilbert, Duncan Lindsay, Sarah Pattison, Sarah Williams

With thanks to Sharon Gulliver and Glenn Rogers for the proofreading.

With thanks to Jan Greenway for the copyright research.

Cover and Graphics used throughout the book © www.edu-clips.com
Clipart from Corel®

50 pence coin © iStock.com/duncan1890
20 pence coin © iStock.com/Jaap2
10 pence coin © iStock.com/john shepherd
5 pence coin © iStock.com/duncan1890
2 pence coin © iStock.com/peterspiro
1 pence coin © iStock.com/coopder1

Printed by W&G Baird Ltd, Antrim.
Based on the classic CGP style created by Richard Parsons.

Text, design, layout and original illustrations© Coordination Group Publications Ltd. (CGP) 2020
All rights reserved.

Photocopying this book is not permitted, even if you have a CLA licence.
Extra copies are available from CGP with next day delivery • 0800 1712 712 • www.cgpbooks.co.uk

How to Use this Book

- This book contains 60 daily practice tests.

- We've split them into 12 sections — that's roughly one for each week of the Year 1 Summer term.

- Each week is made up of 5 tests, so there's one for every school day of the term (Monday – Friday).

- Each test should take about 10 minutes to complete.

- The tests contain a mix of topics from Year 1 Maths. New Year 1 topics are gradually introduced as you go through the book.

- The tests increase in difficulty as you progress through the term.

- Each test looks something like this:

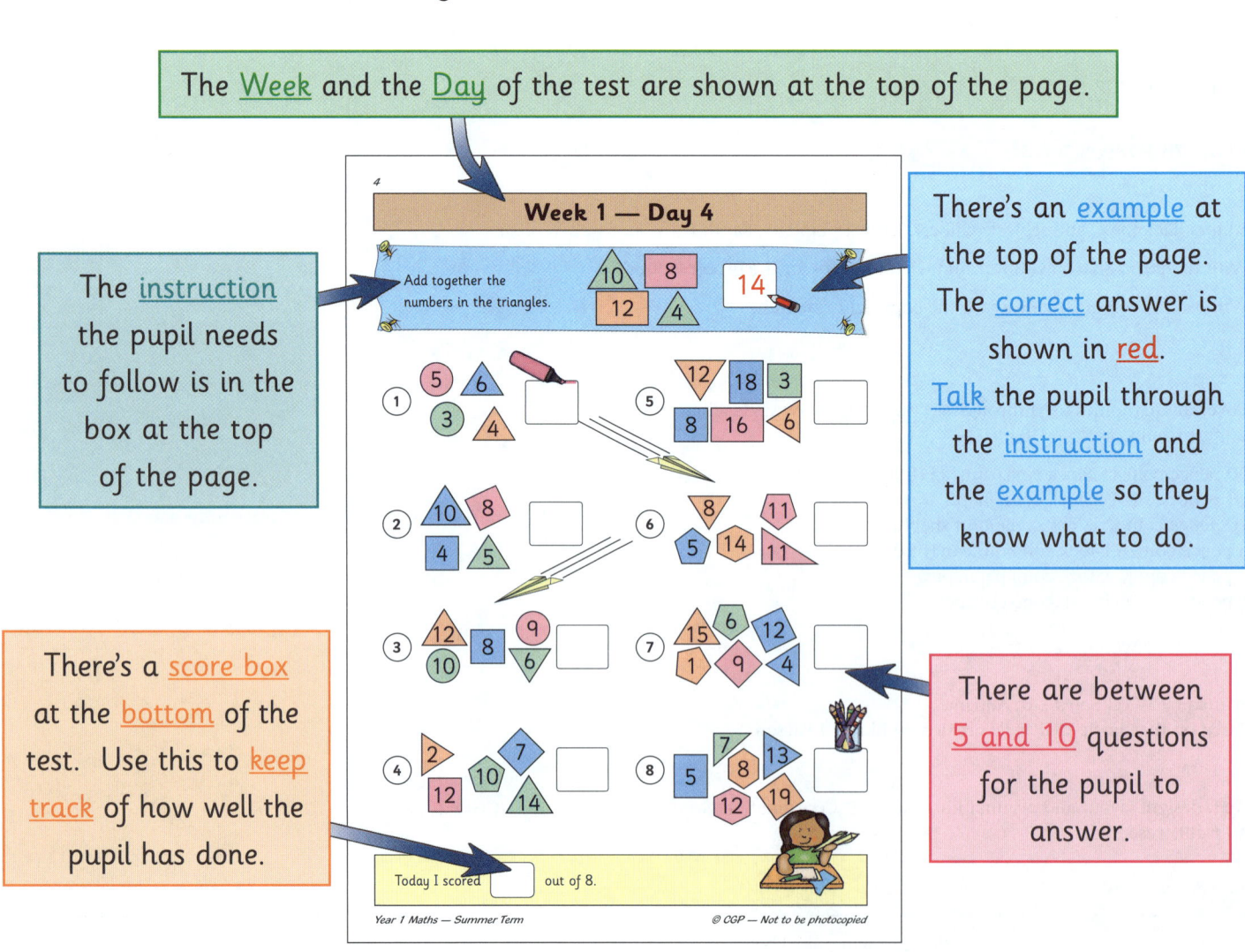

Week 1 — Day 1

Fill in the gap with 'heavier' or 'lighter'.

A shoe is **lighter** than a house.

1) A horse is _____ than a beetle.

2) A book is _____ than a button.

3) A nail is _____ than a hammer.

4) A chair is _____ than a feather.

5) An ant is _____ than a rabbit.

6) A pen is _____ than a sword.

7) A van is _____ than a bicycle.

8) A pear is _____ than a whale.

Today I scored ____ out of 8.

Week 1 — Day 2

Circle the sum that equals the number in the green square.

8 + 3   ~~3 + 9~~   12
11 + 5

1) 6 + 6   7 + 3   10
   11 + 1

2) 9 + 5   16 + 3   13
   11 + 2

3) 7 + 7   0 + 12   14
   9 + 3

4) 10 + 6   9 + 2   11
   6 + 6

5) 11 + 5   8 + 3   16
   7 + 5

6) 4 + 8   9 + 7   15
   12 + 3

7) 14 + 6   1 + 17   20
   12 + 9

8) 12 + 9   8 + 8   18
   5 + 13

9) 15 + 7   11 + 9   19
   3 + 16

10) 15 + 2   3 + 12   17
    13 + 6

Today I scored ☐ out of 10.

Week 1 — Day 3

Fill in the answer. Use the pictures to help you.

$4 \times 2 = \boxed{8}$

①  $2 \times 1 = \boxed{}$

② $2 \times 2 = \boxed{}$

③ $5 \times 2 = \boxed{}$

④ 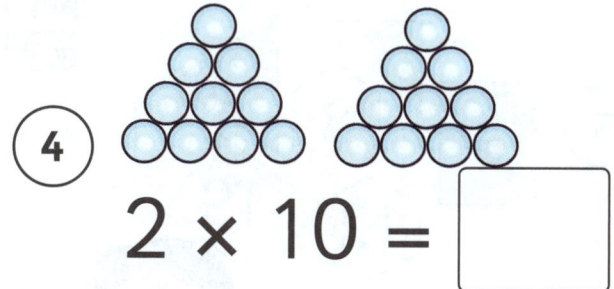 $2 \times 10 = \boxed{}$

⑤ 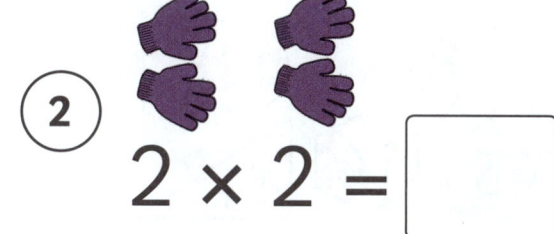 $6 \times 2 = \boxed{}$

⑥ $2 \times 8 = \boxed{}$

⑦ 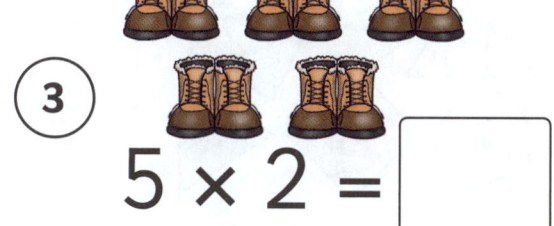 $2 \times 9 = \boxed{}$

⑧  $7 \times 2 = \boxed{}$

Today I scored $\boxed{}$ out of 8.

Week 1 — Day 4

Add together the numbers in the triangles.

Example: Triangle 10, Rectangle 8, Rectangle 12, Triangle 4 → **14**

1) 5 (circle), 6 (triangle), 3 (circle), 4 (triangle)

2) 10 (triangle), 8 (square), 4 (square), 5 (triangle)

3) 12 (triangle), 8 (square), 9 (circle), 10 (circle), 6 (triangle)

4) 2 (triangle), 7 (square), 10 (pentagon), 12 (square), 14 (triangle)

5) 12 (triangle), 18 (square), 3 (square), 8 (rectangle), 16 (rectangle), 6 (triangle)

6) 8 (triangle), 11 (pentagon), 5 (pentagon), 14 (hexagon), 11 (triangle)

7) 15 (triangle), 6 (pentagon), 12 (square), 1 (pentagon), 9 (square), 4 (triangle)

8) 7 (triangle), 13 (triangle), 5 (square), 8 (hexagon), 12 (hexagon), 19 (square)

Today I scored ☐ out of 8.

Year 1 Maths — Summer Term

Week 1 — Day 5

Fill in the missing number. Use the pictures to help you.

 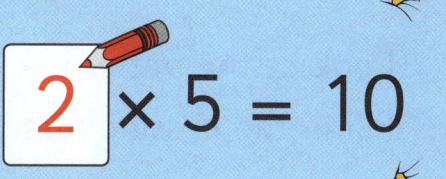

2 × 5 = 10

1)  ☐ × 5 = 5

2)  ☐ × 5 = 15

3) ☐ × 5 = 25

4)  ☐ × 5 = 40

5) ☐ × 5 = 45

6)  ☐ × 5 = 35

Today I scored ☐ out of 6.

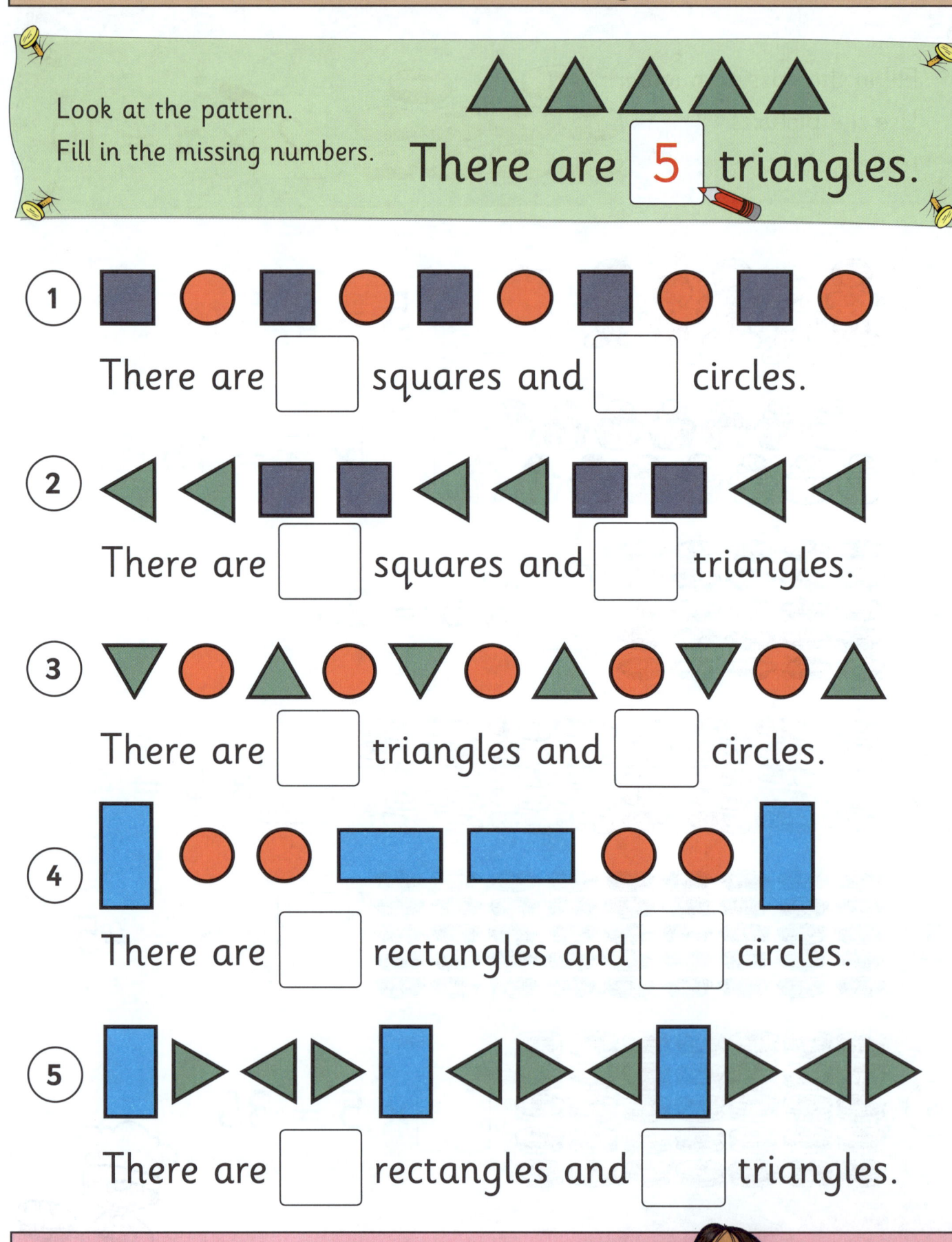

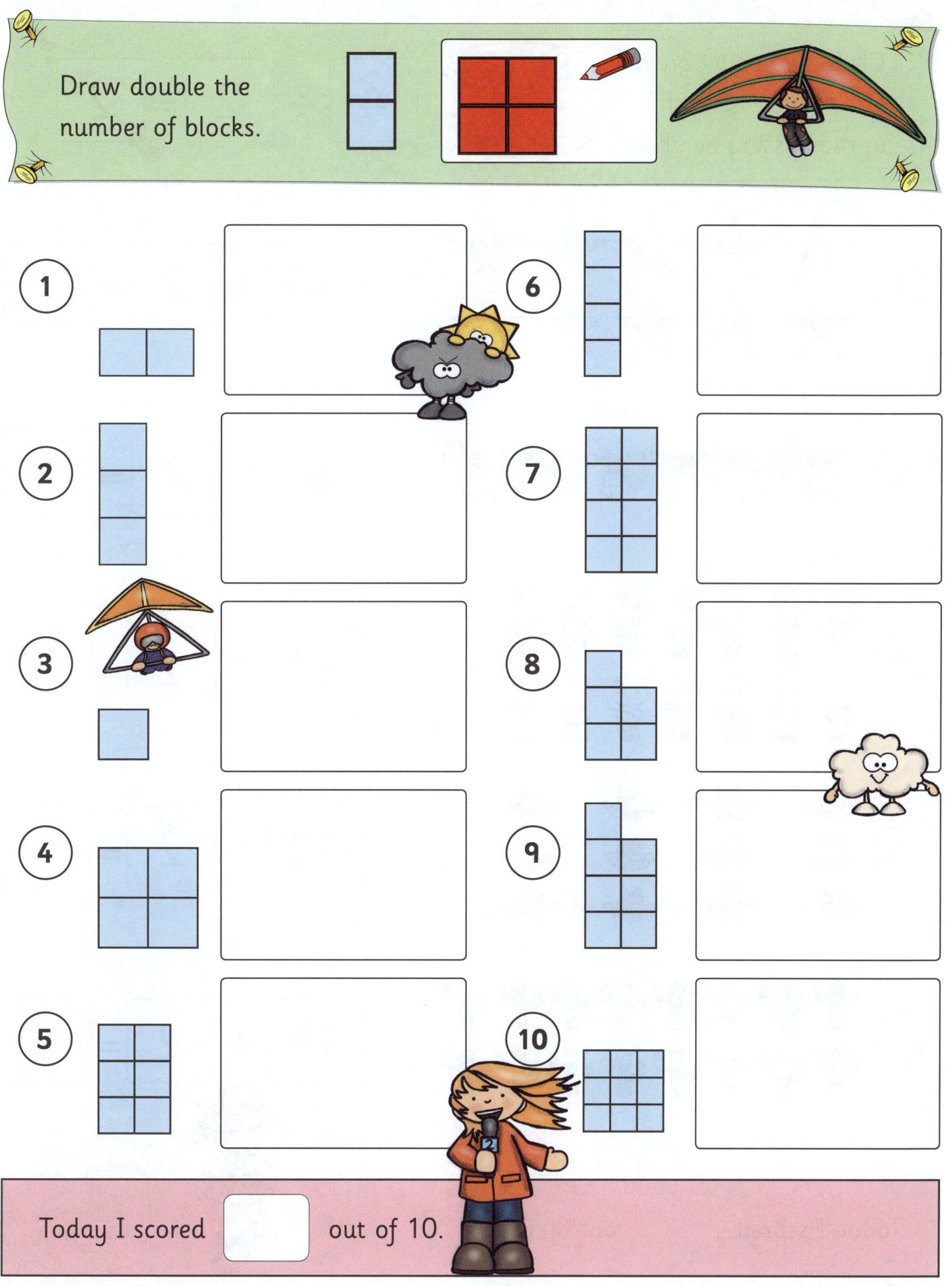

Week 2 — Day 3

Circle two equal groups. Use the groups to fill in the missing number.

1. $10 \div 2 = \square$

2. $6 \div 2 = \square$

3. $14 \div 2 = \square$

4. $12 \div 2 = \square$

5. $16 \div 2 = \square$

Today I scored ☐ out of 10.

Week 2 — Day 4

Fill in the missing number. $\boxed{4} + 4 = 8$

1) $\boxed{} - 4 = 6$

2) $\boxed{} + 5 = 6$

3) $\boxed{} + 2 = 7$

4) $\boxed{} - 3 = 10$

5) $\boxed{} + 5 = 9$

6) $\boxed{} - 6 = 12$

7) $\boxed{} - 4 = 11$

8) $\boxed{} + 15 = 19$

9) $\boxed{} - 7 = 9$

10) $\boxed{} + 8 = 20$

Today I scored $\boxed{}$ out of 10.

Week 2 — Day 5

The buttons are shared equally between 2 people. How many do they each get?

1.
   _____ each

2.
   _____ each

3.
   _____ each

4.
   _____ each

5.
   _____ each

6.
   _____ each

7.
   _____ each

8.
   _____ each

Today I scored _____ out of 8.

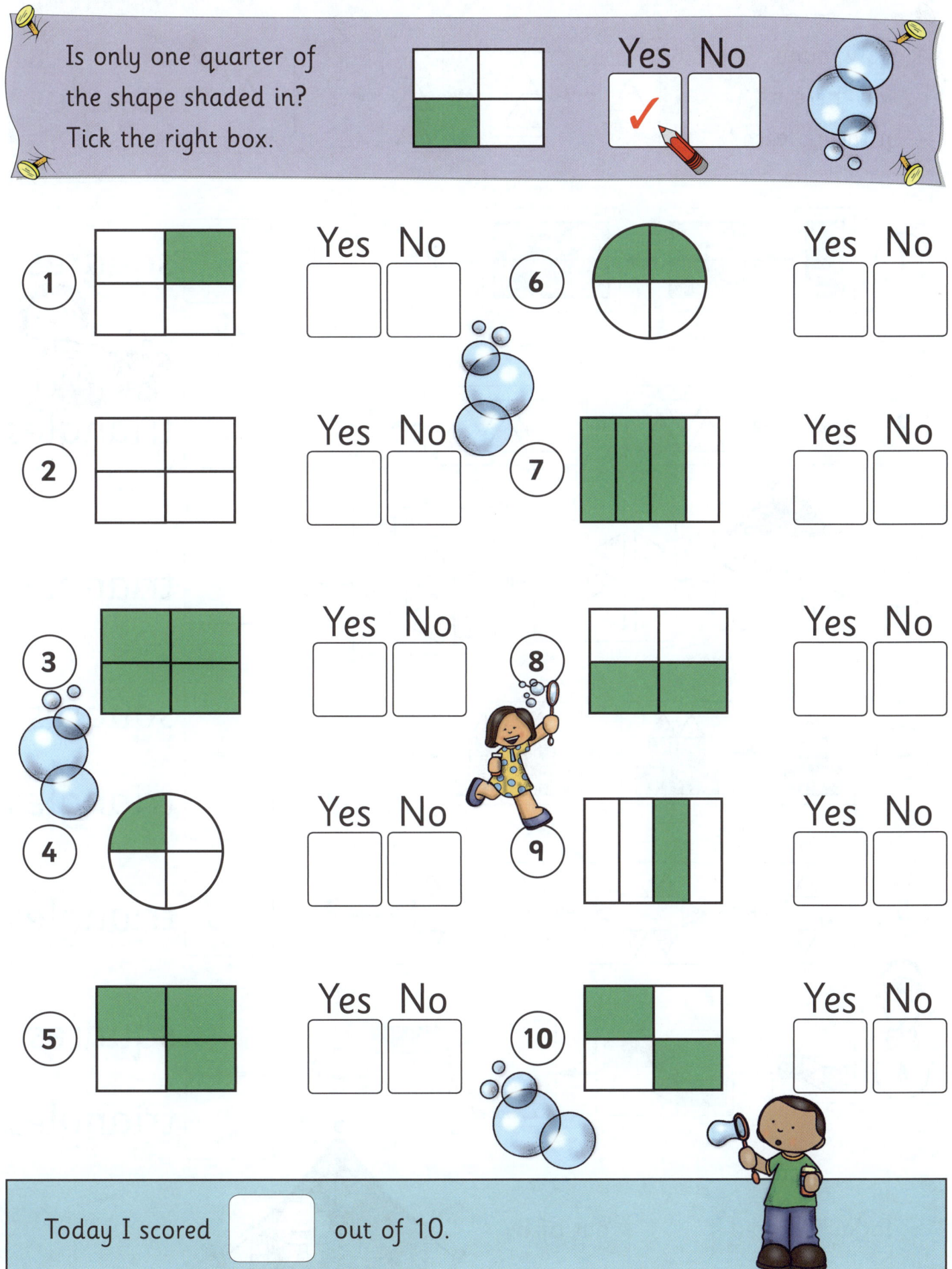

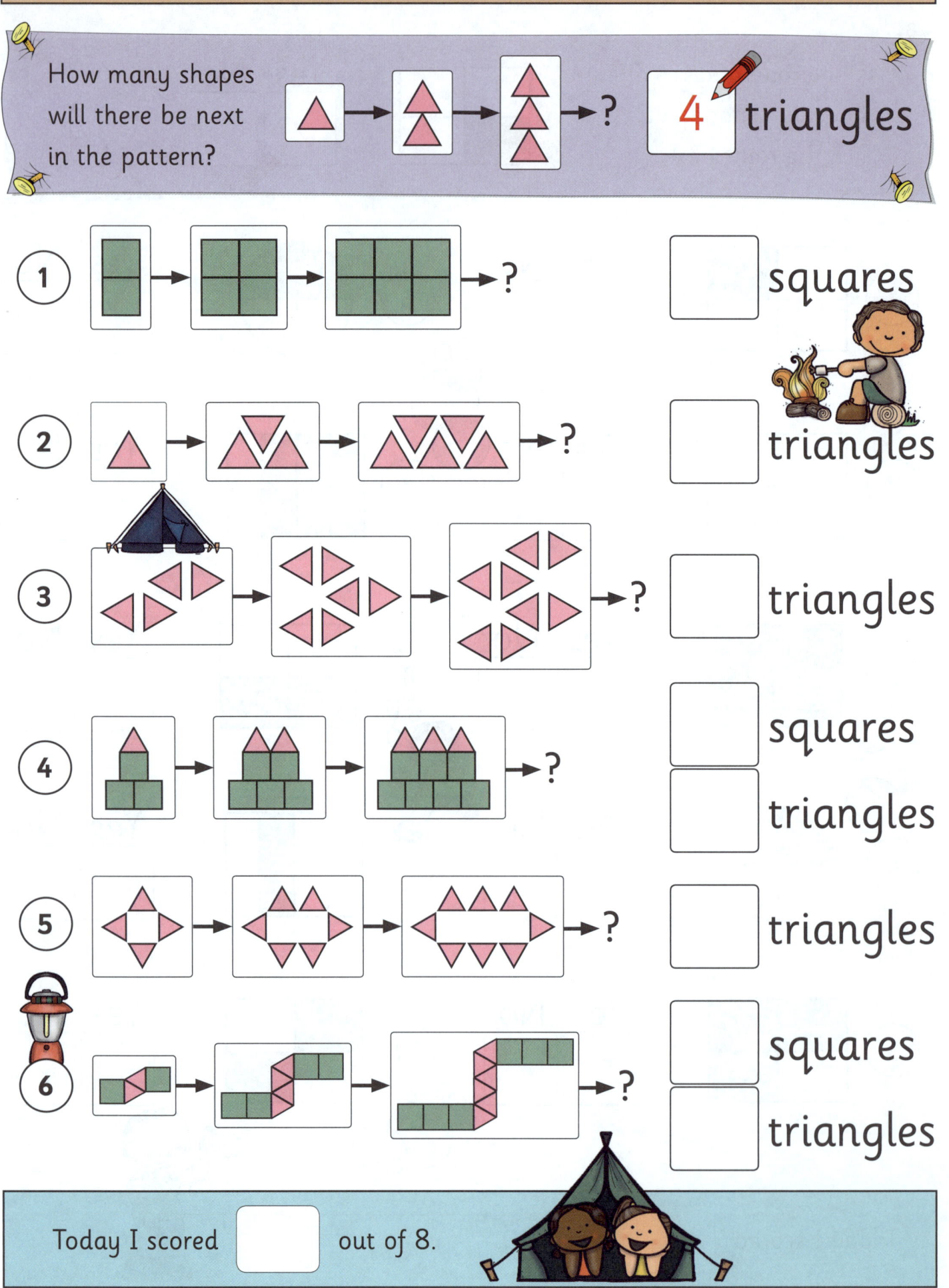

Week 3 — Day 5

Circle 4 equal groups. Use the groups to fill in the missing number.

One quarter of 8 is 2

1  One quarter of 4 is

2 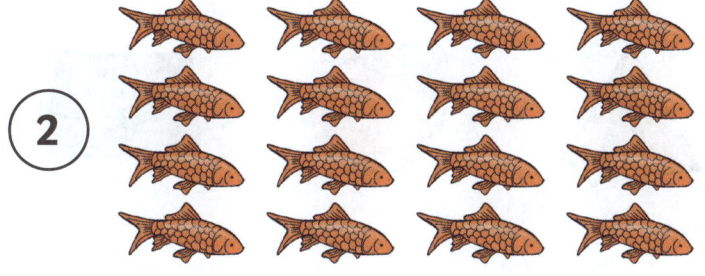 One quarter of 16 is

3  One quarter of 12 is

4 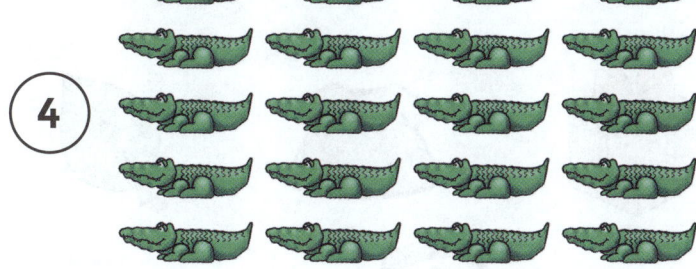 One quarter of 20 is

Today I scored 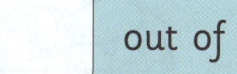 out of 8.

Week 4 — Day 1

Circle the cube. Cross out the sphere.

1)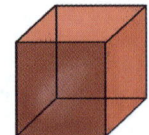

2)

3)

4)

5)

Today I scored ☐ out of 10.

Year 1 Maths — Summer Term

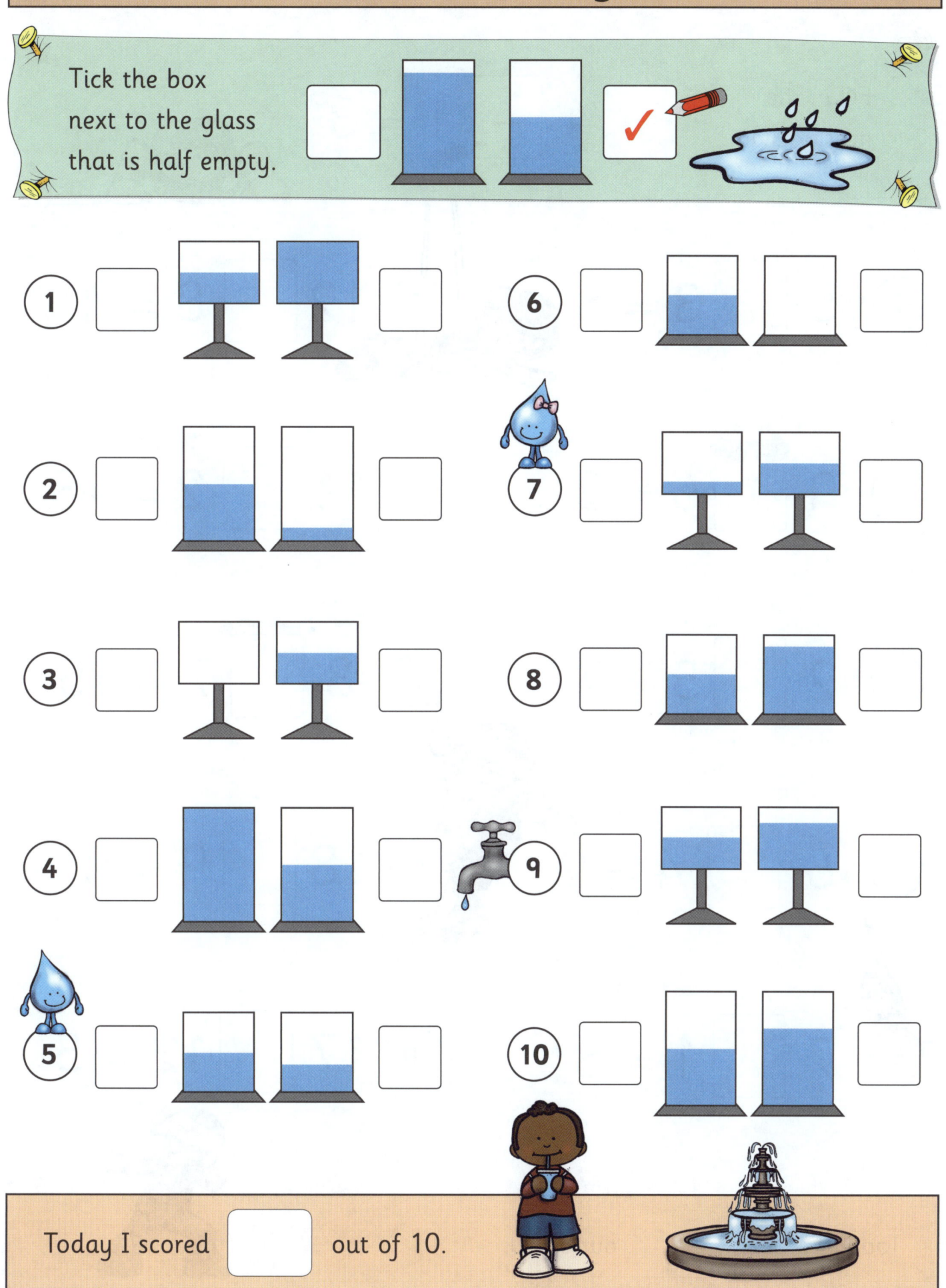

Week 4 — Day 3

Fill in the missing sign. 4 − 1 = 3

1) 5 ☐ 3 = 8

2) 9 ☐ 6 = 3

3) 2 ☐ 5 = 7

4) 6 ☐ 4 = 2

5) 7 ☐ 1 = 8

6) 12 ☐ 8 = 4

7) 11 ☐ 2 = 13

8) 8 ☐ 7 = 15

9) 18 ☐ 9 = 9

10) 17 ☐ 12 = 5

Today I scored ☐ out of 10.

Week 4 — Day 4

Write the total amount of each shape.

2 cubes **2** spheres

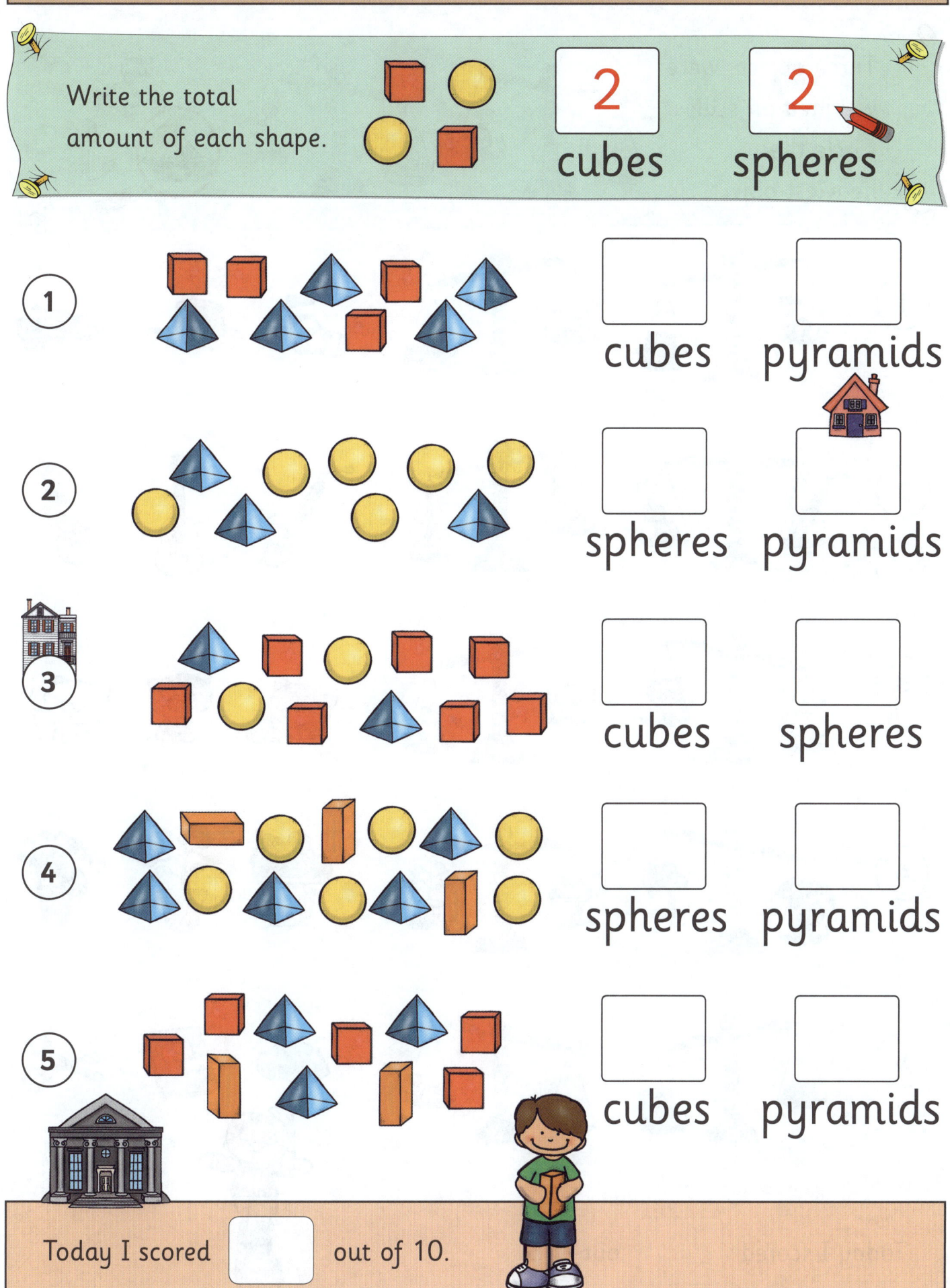

1. ☐ cubes ☐ pyramids
2. ☐ spheres ☐ pyramids
3. ☐ cubes ☐ spheres
4. ☐ spheres ☐ pyramids
5. ☐ cubes ☐ pyramids

Today I scored ☐ out of 10.

Week 4 — Day 5

Three objects were weighed on scales. Circle the heaviest object.

1.

2.

3.

4.

5.

Today I scored ☐ out of 5.

Week 5 — Day 1

Fill in the answer.   1 add 11 equals 12

1) 18 subtract 2 equals ☐

2) 3 add 16 equals ☐

3) 14 add 5 equals ☐

4) 17 subtract 4 equals ☐

5) 10 add 0 equals ☐

6) 13 subtract 12 equals ☐

7) 6 add 11 equals ☐

8) 9 add 3 equals ☐

9) 7 add 8 equals ☐

10) 15 subtract 9 equals ☐

Today I scored ☐ out of 10.

Week 5 — Day 2

Look at the items.

Cross out the item between the drink and the hat.

Circle the item next to the sunglasses on the right.

1

2

3

4

5

Today I scored ☐ out of 10.

Year 1 Maths — Summer Term

Week 5 — Day 3

Toni and George want to split the biscuits equally. How many biscuits do they each get?

4

1. 
2. 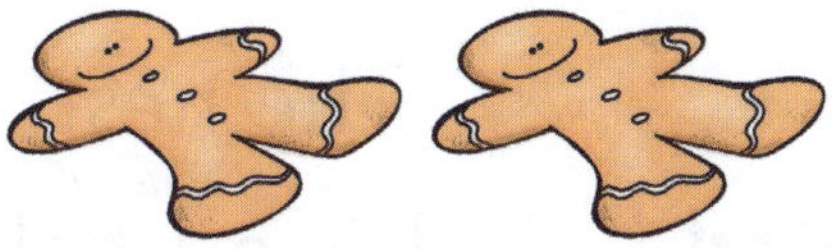 
3. 
4. 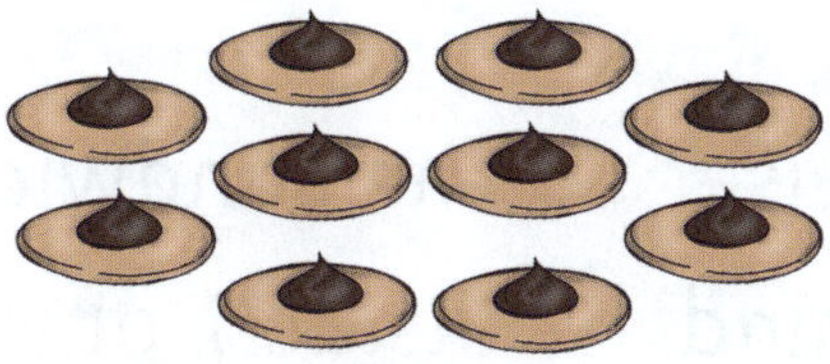
5.  
6. 
7. 
8. 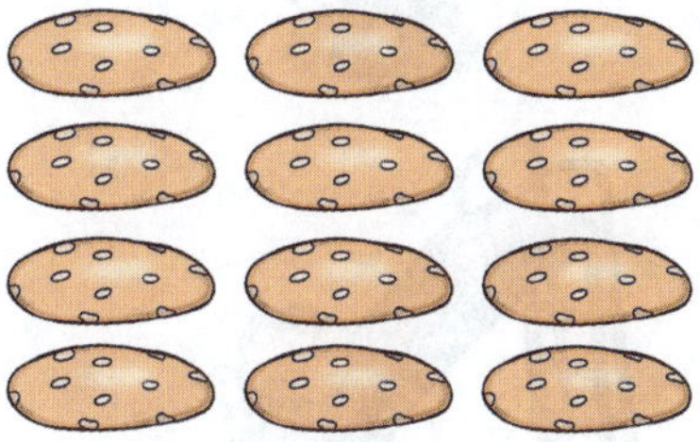 
9. 
10.

Today I scored ☐ out of 10.

Week 5 — Day 4

Look at the picture. Circle the right word in each sentence.

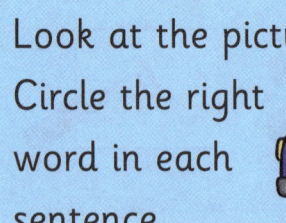

The bird is (above) / below the truck.

The person is outside / (inside) the truck.

1)

The crayons are inside / outside the box.

The ruler is in front of / behind the box.

2)

The deer is in front of / behind the tree.

The nest is above / below the deer.

3)

The ball is above / below the slide.

The person is in front of / behind the slide.

4)

The notebook is in front of / behind the bag.

The sandwich is inside / outside the bag.

5)

The person is inside / outside the tent.

The flag is above / below the person.

Today I scored ☐ out of 10.

Week 5 — Day 5

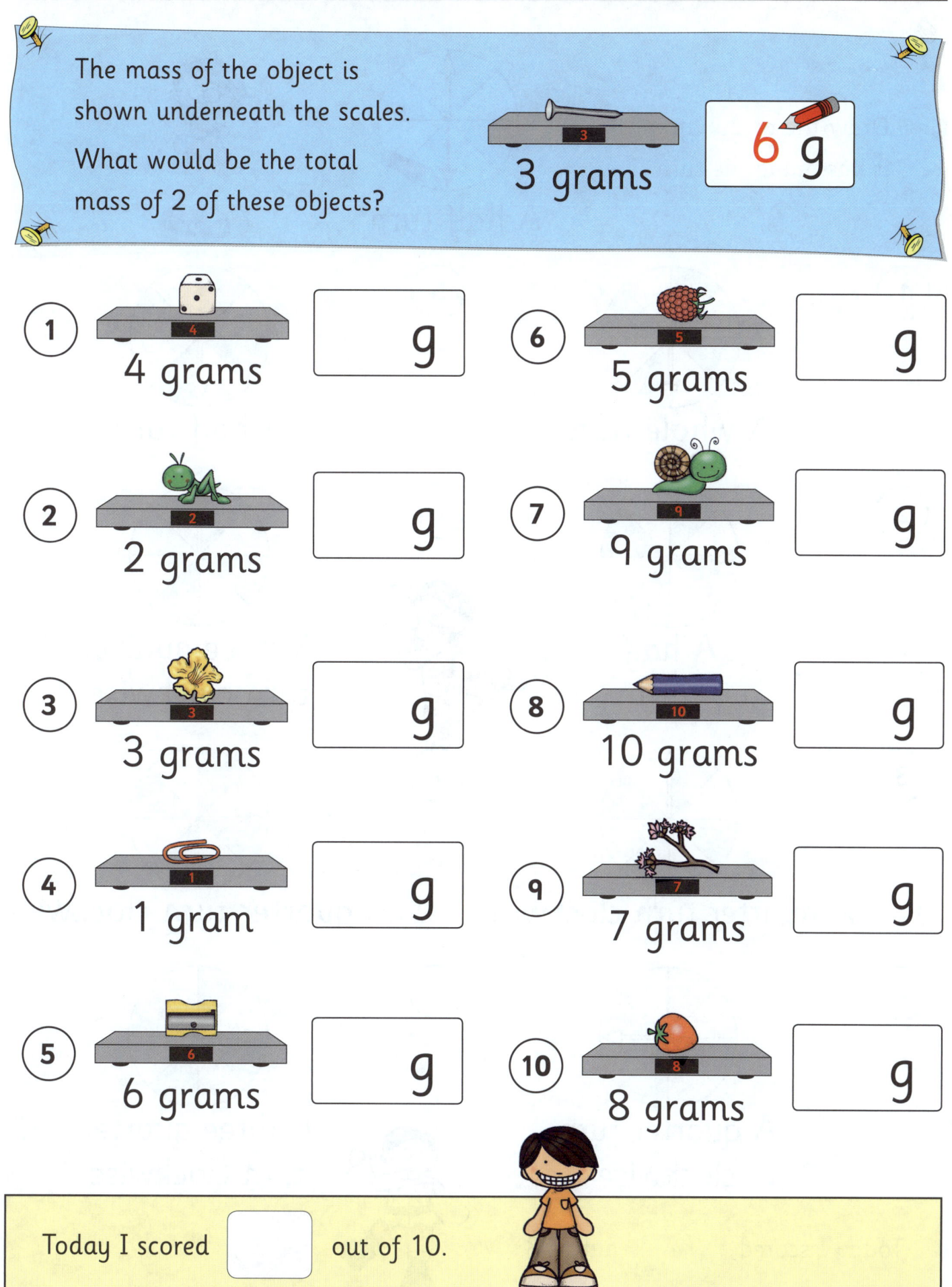

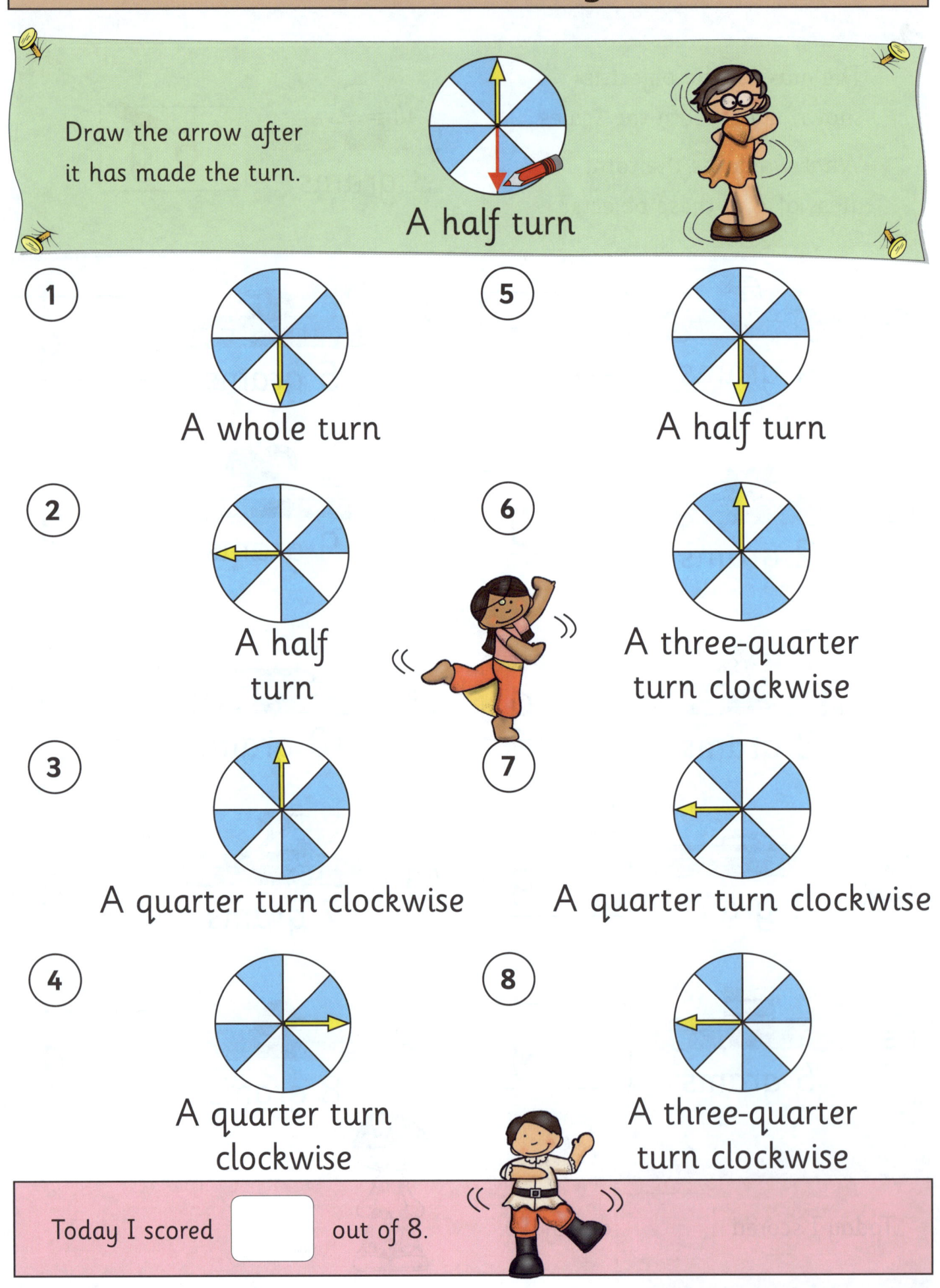

Week 6 — Day 2

Work out the answer. 10 + 2 = 12

1) 13 − 1 =

6) 18 − 0 =

2) 5 + 10 =

7) 19 − 3 =

3) 7 + 11 =

8) 14 + 5 =

4) 12 + 4 =

9) 20 − 7 =

5) 20 + 0 =

10) 16 + 4 =

Today I scored ☐ out of 10.

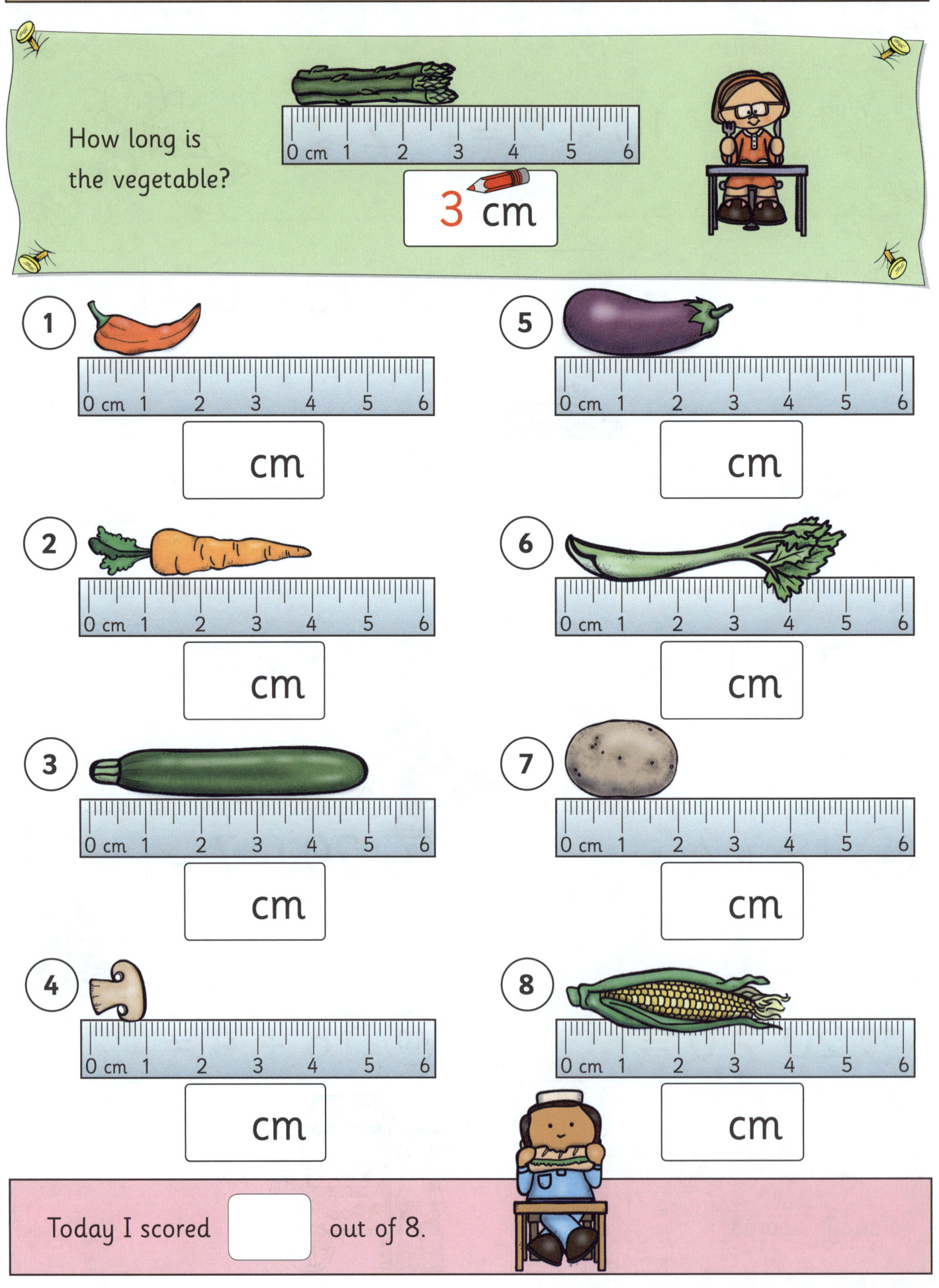

Week 6 — Day 4

How many items does the person have altogether?

Keith has 3 flowers.
He buys 12 more.

15

1) Malik has 10 eggs.
He buys 4 more.

2) Bonnie has 18 jars.
She is given 1 more.

3) Tanisha wears 3 hats.
She puts on 14 more.
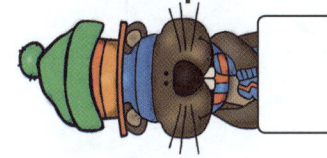

4) Abid carries 16 bags.
He picks up 2 more.

5) Paul has 11 coins.
He finds 8 more.

6) Nel has 15 cups.
She buys 4 more.

7) Dean has 6 twigs.
He picks up 13 more.

8) Isla has 3 sweets.
She buys 17 more.

Today I scored ☐ out of 8.

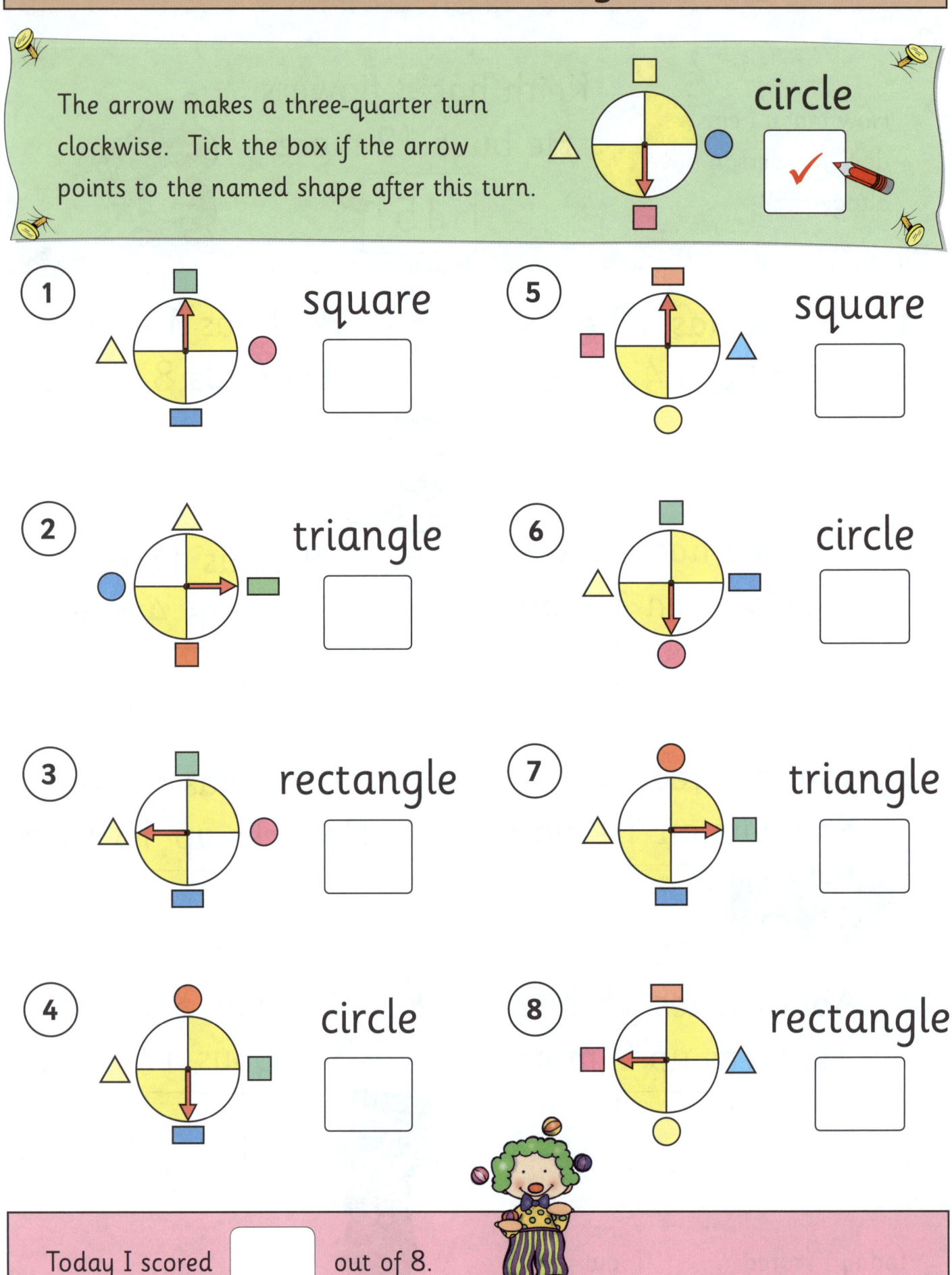

Week 7 — Day 1

Draw an arrow on the scale to show the right mass.

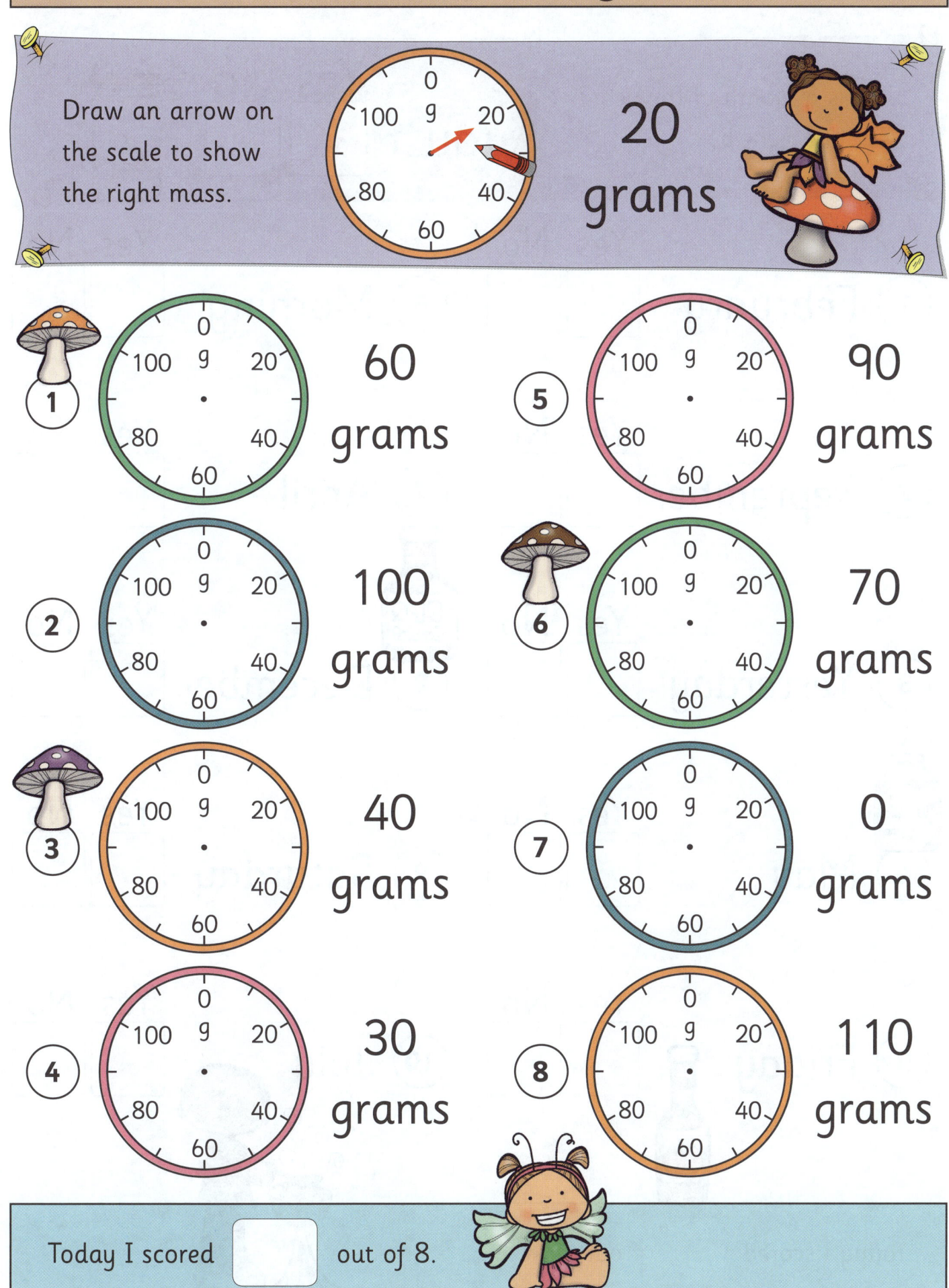

1. 60 grams
2. 100 grams
3. 40 grams
4. 30 grams
5. 90 grams
6. 70 grams
7. 0 grams
8. 110 grams

Today I scored ☐ out of 8.

Week 7 — Day 2

Is this a month of the year? Tick the right box.

August Yes ✓ No ☐

1. February — Yes ☐ No ☐
2. September — Yes ☐ No ☐
3. Yesterday — Yes ☐ No ☐
4. May — Yes ☐ No ☐
5. Friday — Yes ☐ No ☐
6. Morning — Yes ☐ No ☐
7. April — Yes ☐ No ☐
8. December — Yes ☐ No ☐
9. Saturday — Yes ☐ No ☐
10. July — Yes ☐ No ☐

Today I scored ☐ out of 10.

Year 1 Maths — Summer Term

Week 7 — Day 3

Circle any coin that has a value less than the amount shown on the purse.

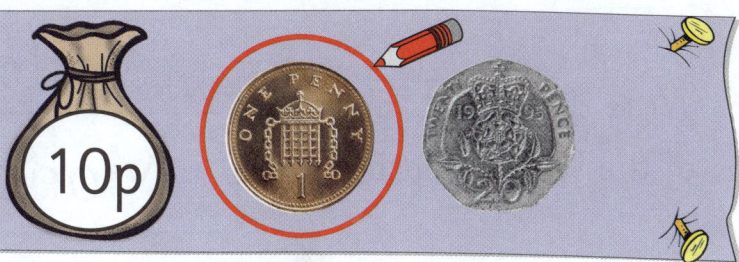

1.

6.

2.

7.

3.

8.

4.

9.

5.

10.

Today I scored ☐ out of 10.

Week 7 — Day 4

Write down the right day of the week in each box.

today	tomorrow
Monday	Tuesday

1. yesterday [ ] ← today [Friday] → tomorrow [ ]

2. yesterday [ ] ← today [Tuesday] → tomorrow [ ]

3. yesterday [ ] ← today [Saturday] → tomorrow [ ]

4. yesterday [Wednesday] ← today [ ] → tomorrow [ ]

5. yesterday [ ] ← today [ ] → tomorrow [Thursday]

Today I scored [ ] out of 10.

Week 8 — Day 1

Anne is 4 blocks tall. How many blocks tall is each fox?  Jo is 1 block shorter than Anne.  3

1) Owen is 2 blocks taller than Anne.

2) Shin is 2 blocks shorter than Anne.

3) Will is 1 block taller than Anne.

4) Mia is the same height as Anne.

5) Nora is 3 blocks shorter than Anne.

6) Luke is 3 blocks taller than Anne.

Today I scored ☐ out of 6.

Week 8 — Day 2

Draw the missing pattern in the box.

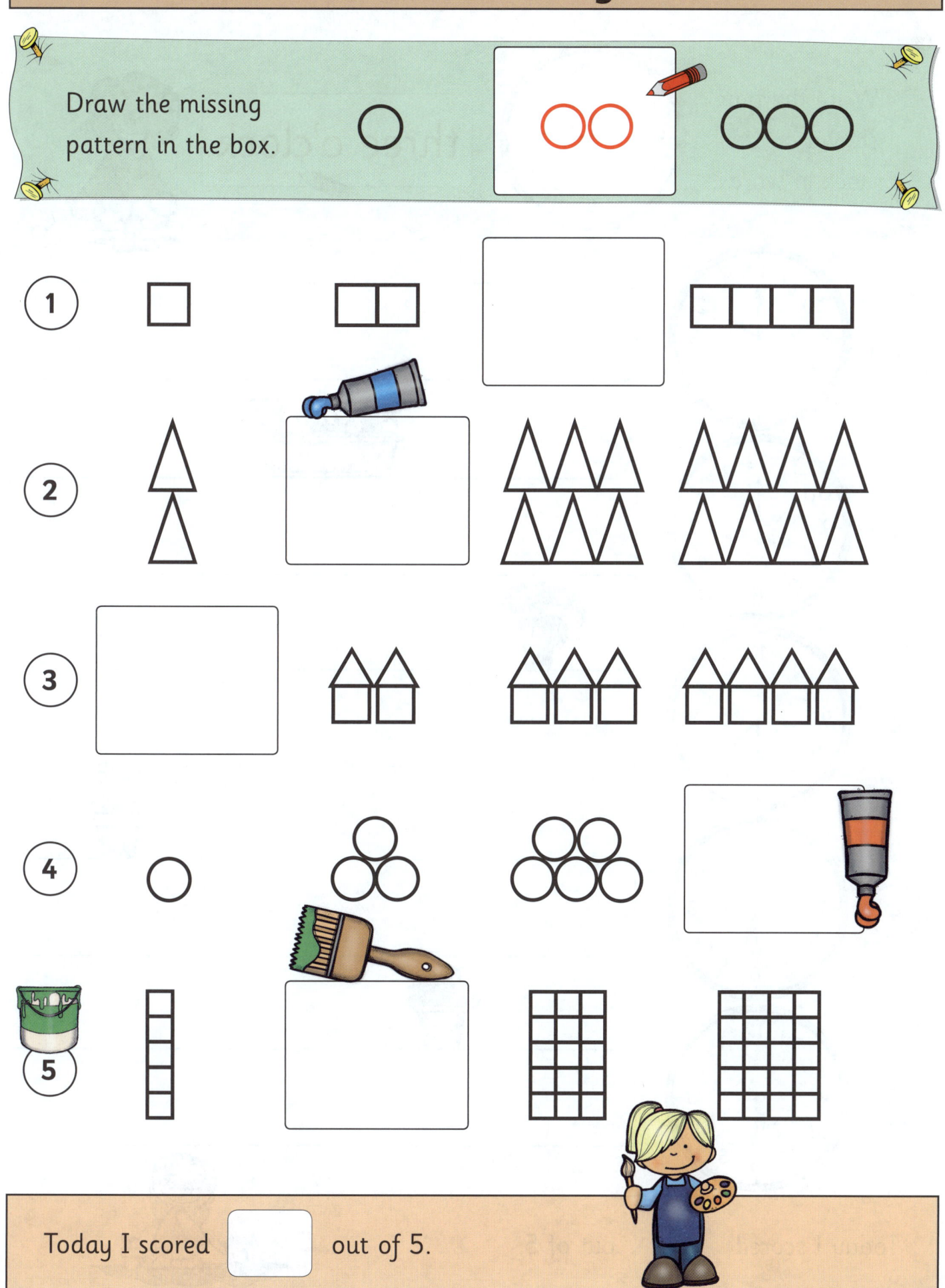

Week 8 — Day 3

Write the time shown on the clock in words. → **three o'clock**

Week 8 — Day 4

What is the missing number?   2 = [3] − 1

1) 2 = ☐ − 2

2) 7 = ☐ − 1

3) 4 = ☐ − 4

4) 2 = ☐ − 4

5) 3 = ☐ − 6

6) 2 = ☐ − 3

7) 3 = ☐ − 5

8) 5 = ☐ − 2

9) 3 = ☐ − 4

10) 2 = ☐ − 7

Today I scored ☐ out of 10.

Week 8 — Day 5

Look at the clock. What time was it one hour ago?  **3** o'clock

1.  ___ o'clock

2.  ___ o'clock

3.  ___ o'clock

4.  ___ o'clock

5.  ___ o'clock

6.  ___ o'clock

7.  ___ o'clock

8.  ___ o'clock

9.  ___ o'clock

10.  ___ o'clock

Today I scored ___ out of 10.

Week 9 — Day 1

Who slept for the longest time?
Circle the right answer.

2 hours   1 hour
(3 hours) ← circled

1) 2 hours   7 hours
    4 hours

2) 5 hours   6 hours
    9 hours

3) 3 hours   8 hours
    5 hours

4) 8 hours   10 hours
    12 hours

5) 9 hours   13 hours
    11 hours

6) 10 hours   11 hours
    15 hours

7) 18 hours   9 hours
    17 hours

8) 14 hours   19 hours
    16 hours

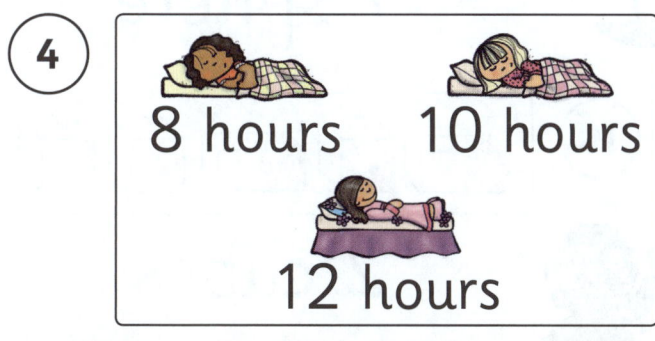

Today I scored [ ] out of 8.

Week 9 — Day 2

Cross out the right shapes.

1 triangle

1.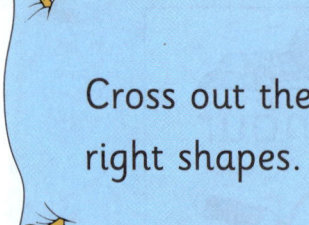

2 circles

2.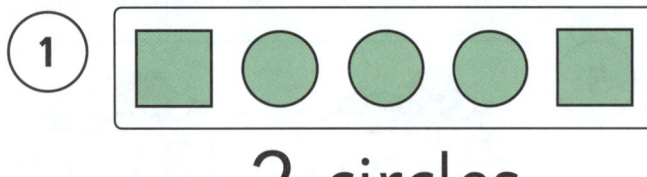

2 rectangles

3.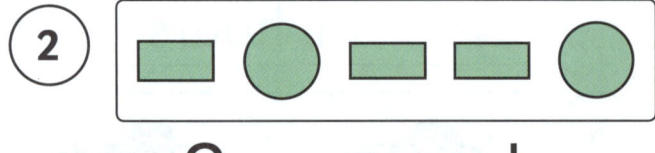

2 triangles

4.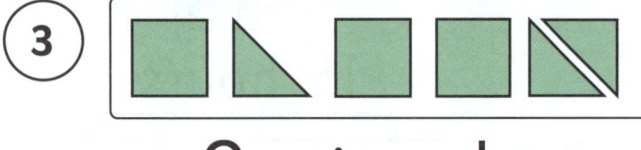

2 squares

5.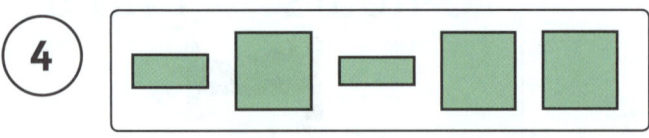

3 rectangles

6.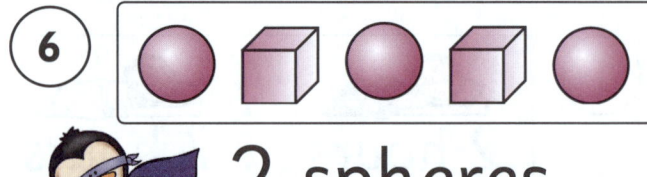

2 spheres

7.

1 cube

8.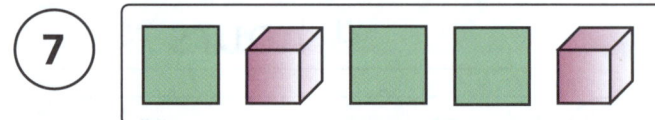

2 pyramids

9.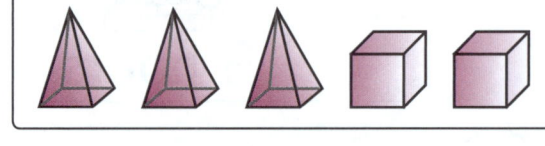

1 sphere

10.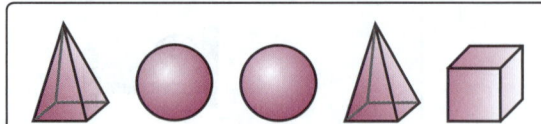

2 cubes

Today I scored ☐ out of 10.

Year 1 Maths — Summer Term

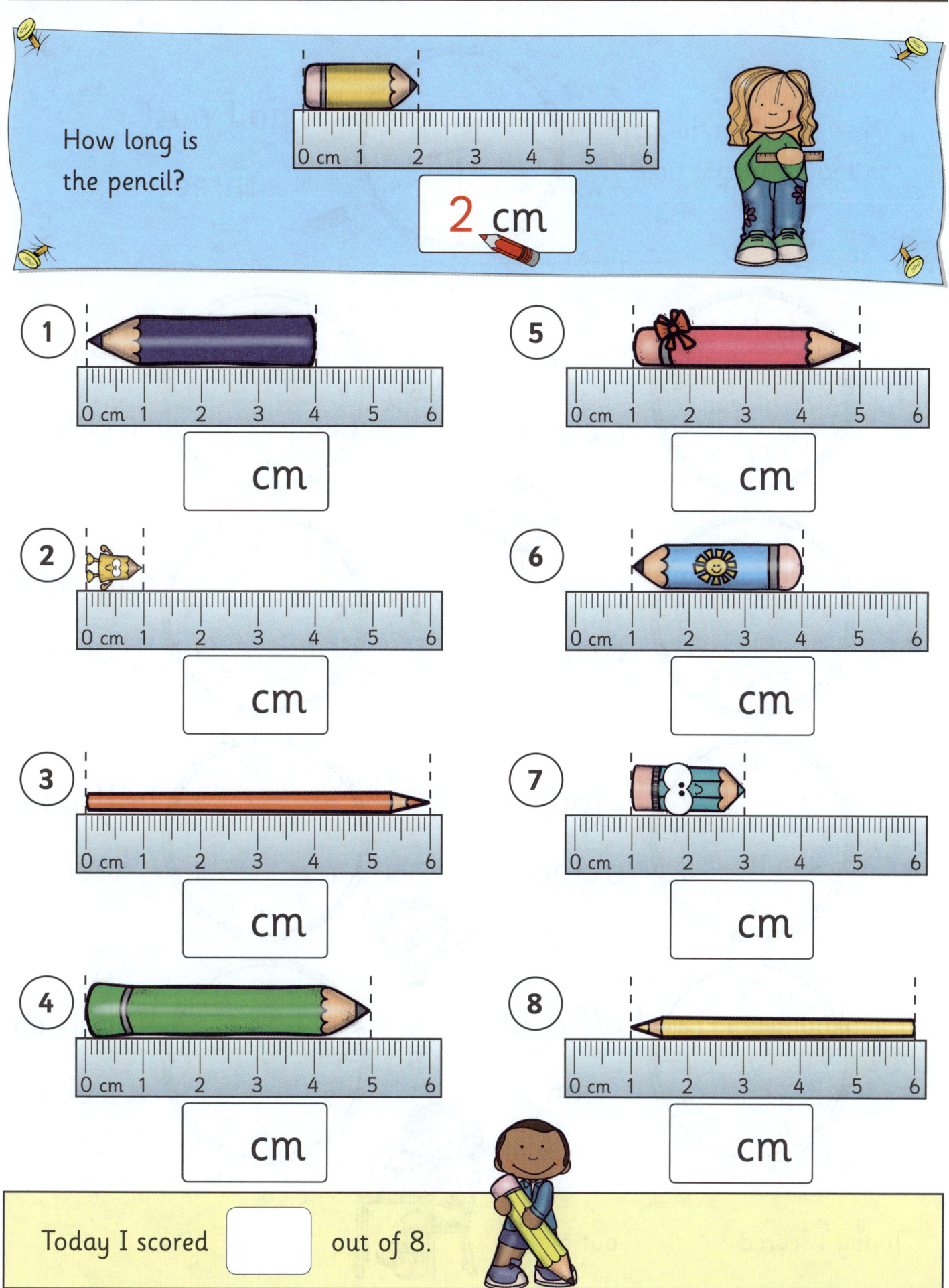

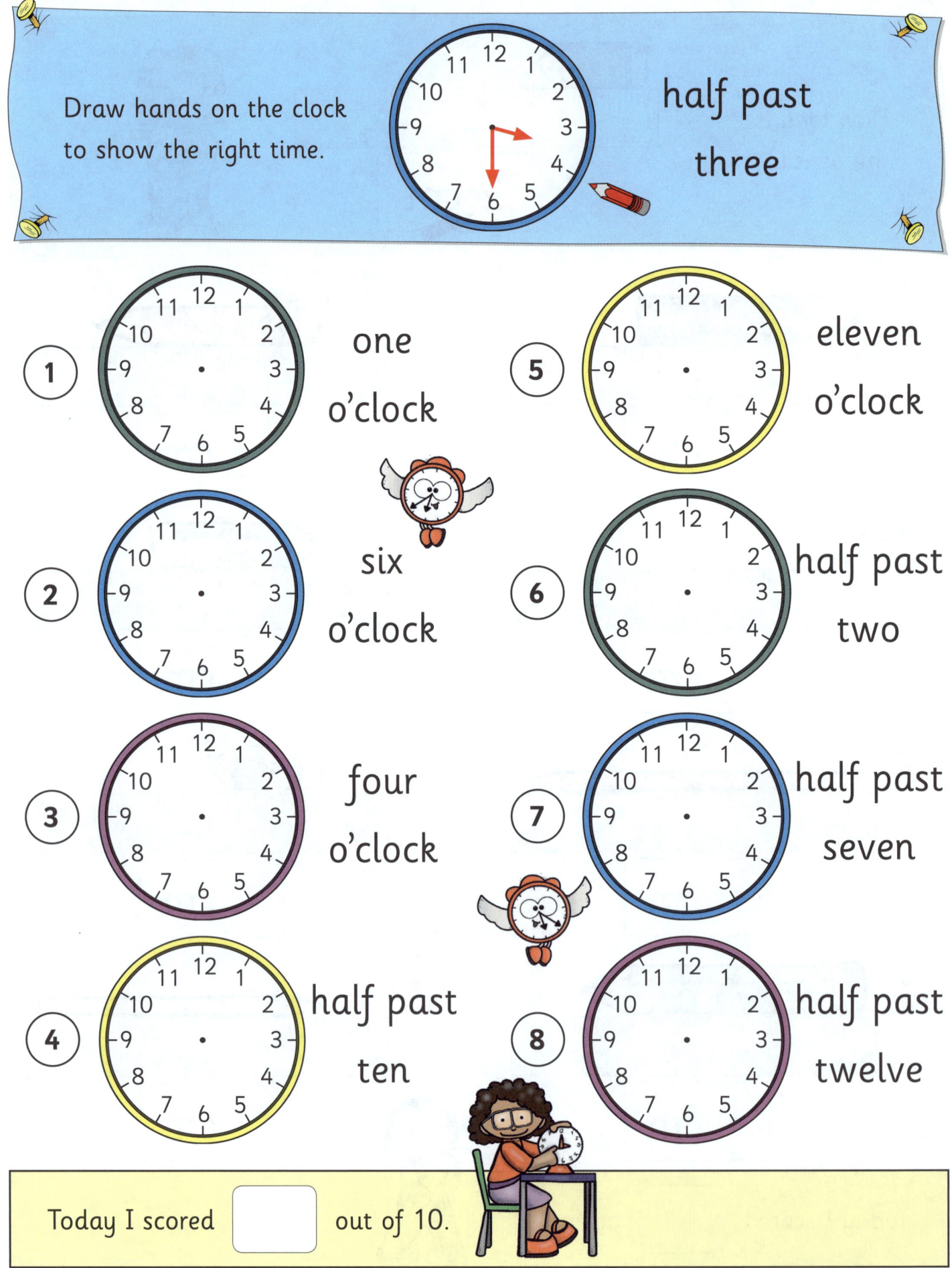

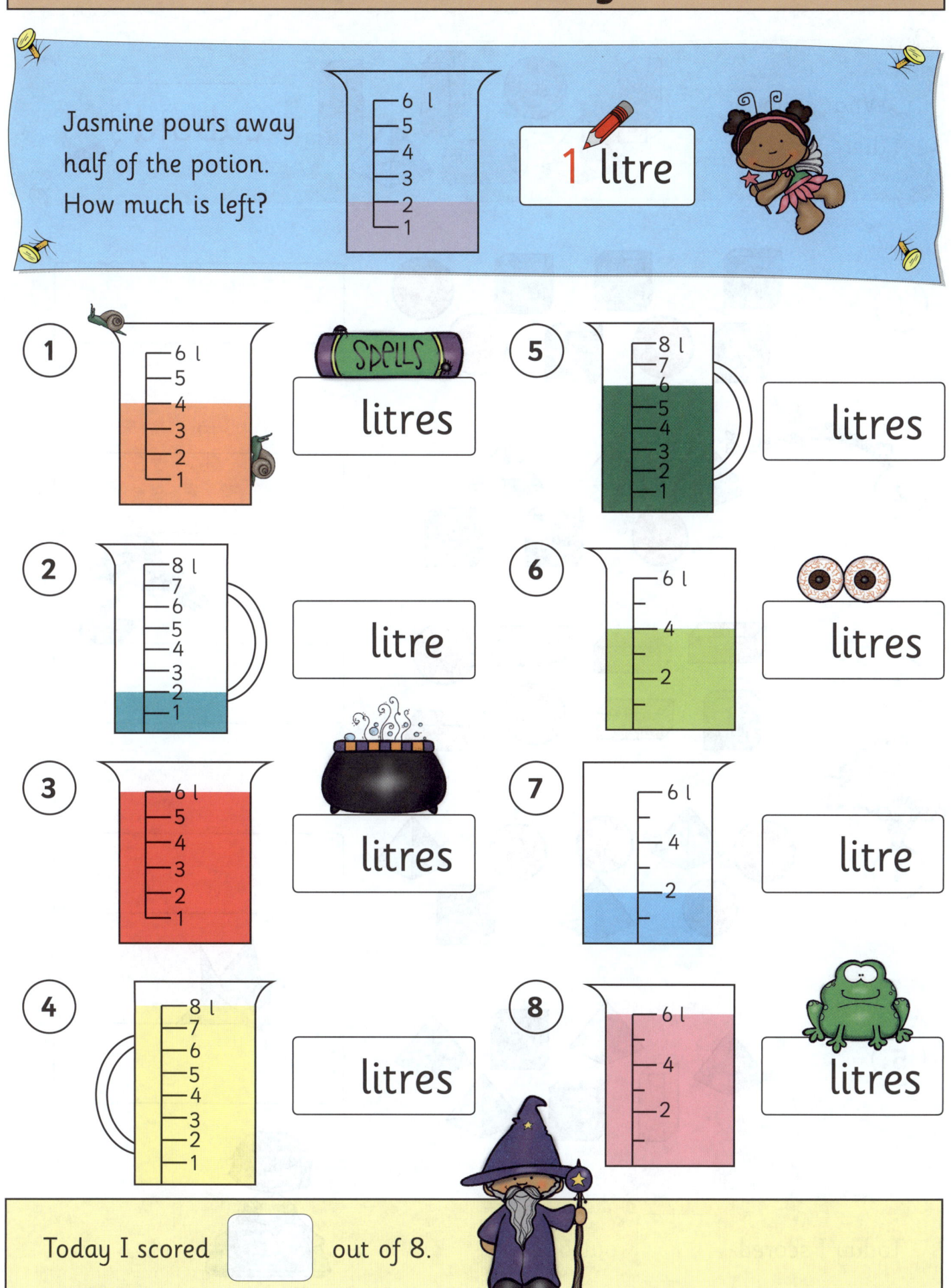

Week 10 — Day 1

What shape is there most of?   **cuboid**

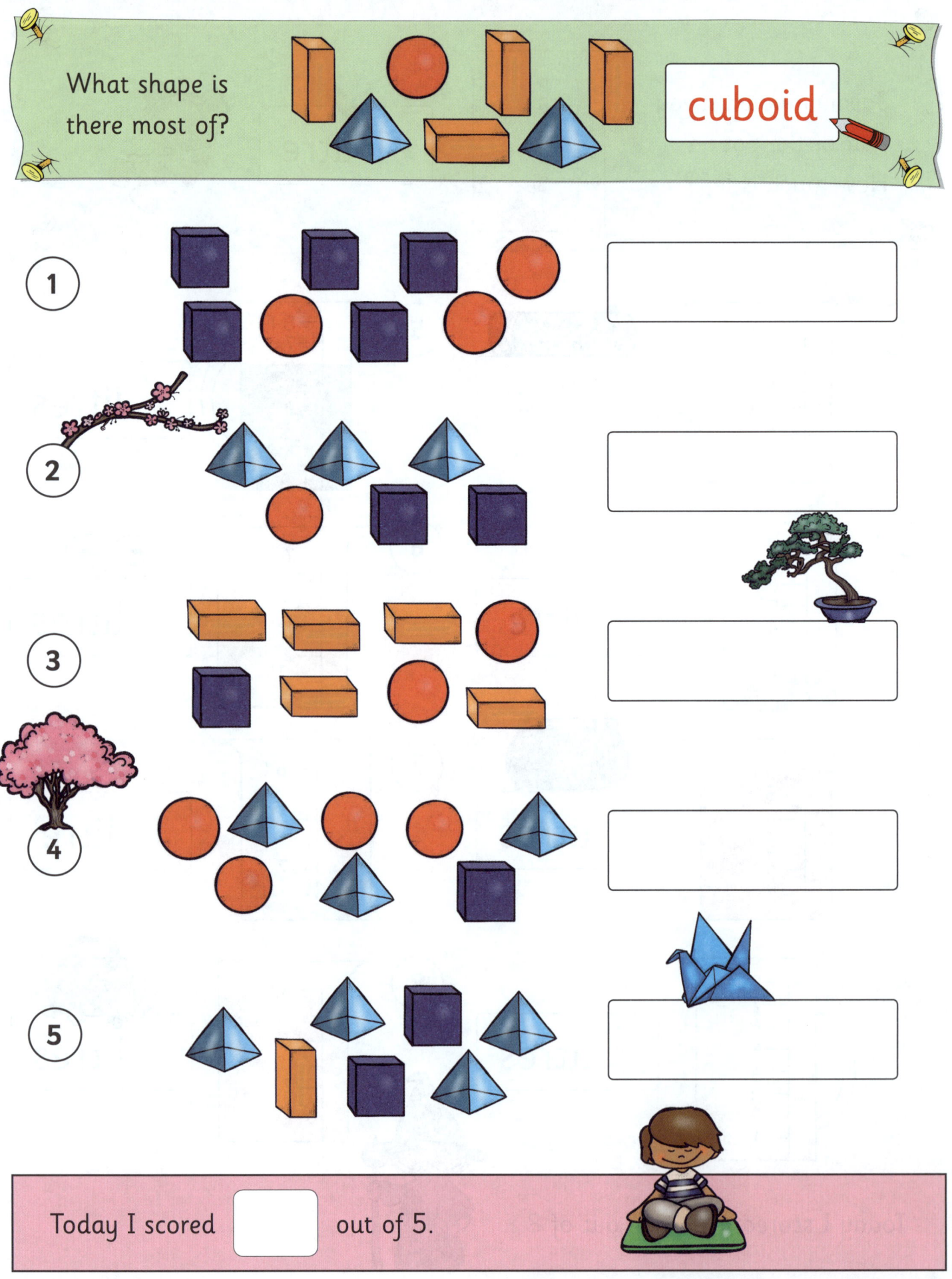

Today I scored ☐ out of 5.

Year 1 Maths — Summer Term

Week 10 — Day 2

Fill in the answer.   13 add 5 equals 18

1) 8 add 1 equals
2) 9 subtract 4 equals
3) 15 subtract 3 equals
4) 7 add 0 equals
5) 17 subtract 6 equals
6) 6 add 14 equals
7) 13 add 4 equals
8) 5 add 8 equals
9) 20 subtract 11 equals
10) 12 subtract 9 equals

Today I scored ☐ out of 10.

Week 10 — Day 3

The direction the object is moving is given. Draw an arrow to show this direction.

forwards

1. backwards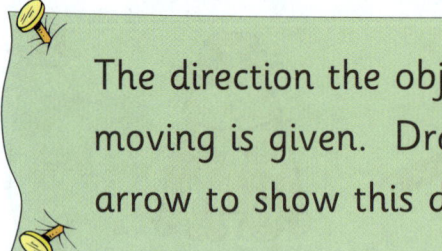

2. up

3. forwards

4. down

5. up

6. down

7. backwards

8. forwards

Today I scored [ ] out of 8.

Week 10 — Day 4

The weather forecast for a city is shown. Today is Thursday. Fill in the right forecast.

 Thursday — rainy
 Friday — cloudy

Tomorrow it will be **cloudy**

1.  Wednesday — stormy | Thursday — cloudy | Friday — rainy

   Today it is ____

2.  Wednesday — rainy | Thursday — rainy | Friday — stormy

   Tomorrow it will be ____

3.  Tuesday — rainy | Wednesday — sunny | Thursday — cloudy

   Two days before today it was ____

4.  Wednesday — snowy | Thursday — rainy | Friday — rainy

   Yesterday it was ____

5.  Thursday — sunny | Friday — cloudy | Saturday — rainy

   Two days after today it will be ____

Today I scored ____ out of 5.

Week 10 — Day 5

Fill in the missing number. Use the pictures to help you.

3 × 2 = 6

1) 2 × 1 =

5) 5 × 2 =

2) 2 × 2 =

6) 4 × 2 =

3) 5 × 1 =

7) 6 × 2 =

4) 2 × 3 =

8) 5 × 3 =

Today I scored [ ] out of 8.

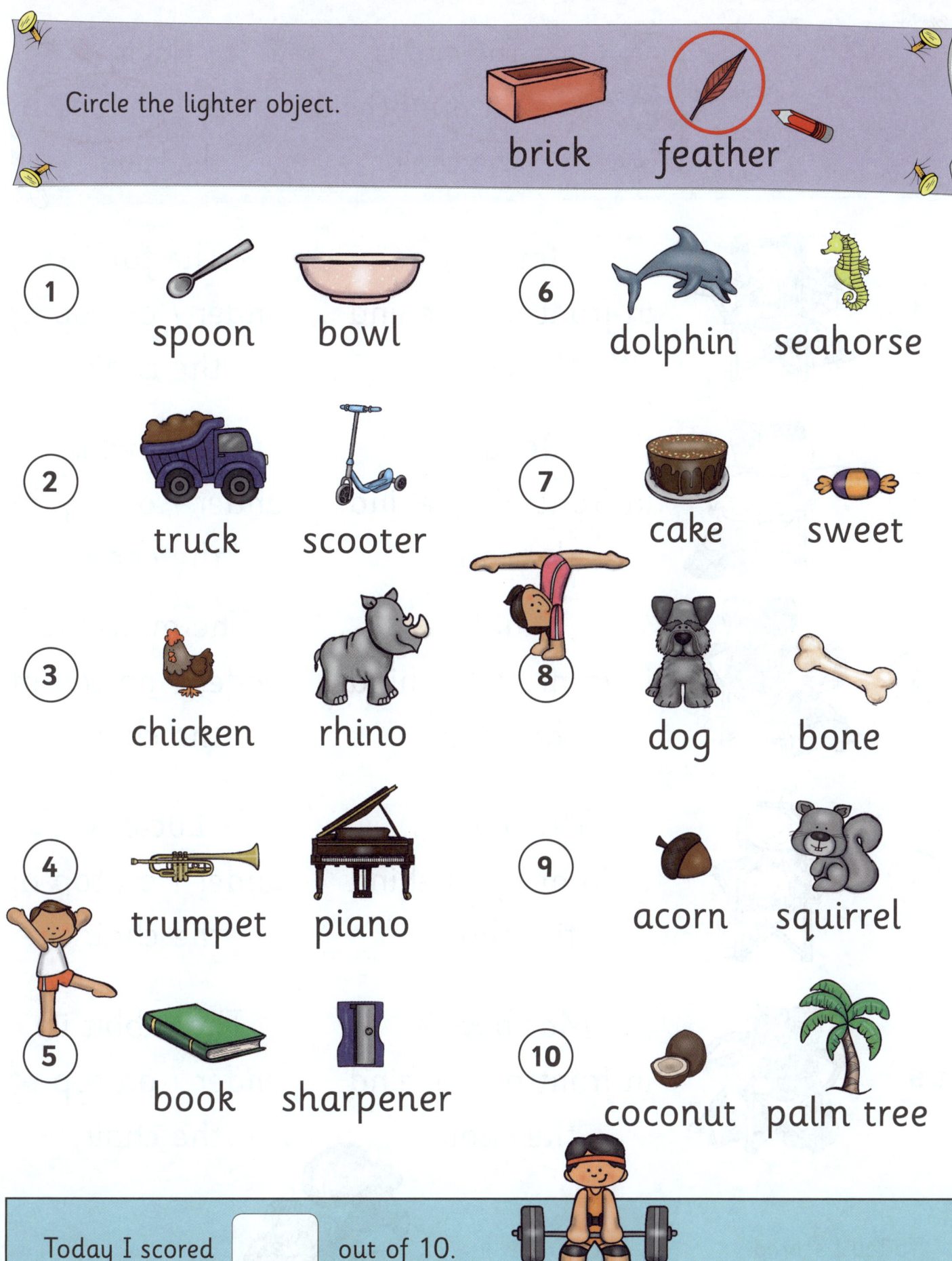

Week 11 — Day 2

Look at the picture. Circle the right phrase in each sentence.

The bird is (in front of) / behind the chair.

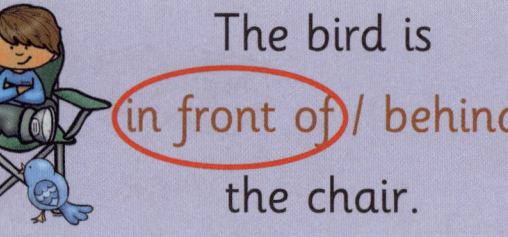

Hal is under / (on top of) the chair.

Iman is in front of / behind the chair.

The fox is under / on top of the chair.

Joey is in front of / behind the chair.

The owl is under / on top of the chair.

Kai is in front of / behind the chair.

The mouse is under / on top of the chair.

The duck is in front of / behind the chair.

Lucie is under / on top of the chair.

Matthew is in front of / behind the chair.

The rabbit is under / on top of the chair.

Today I scored  out of 10.

Year 1 Maths — Summer Term © CGP — Not to be photocopied

Week 11 — Day 3

Fill in the missing sign.   6 **+** 3 = 9

1) 10 ☐ 3 = 7

2) 5 ☐ 11 = 16

3) 6 ☐ 1 = 5

4) 4 ☐ 2 = 6

5) 3 = 7 ☐ 4

6) 15 ☐ 13 = 2

7) 20 = 17 ☐ 3

8) 17 = 19 ☐ 2

9) 7 = 11 ☐ 4

10) 15 = 8 ☐ 7

Today I scored ☐ out of 10.

Week 11 — Day 4

Look at the shapes. Fill in the number of the shape given.

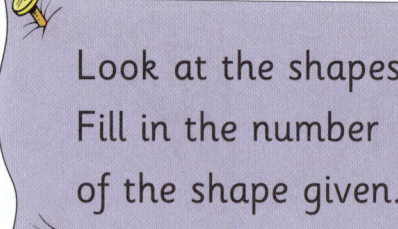 
3 squares

1
triangles

2
circles

3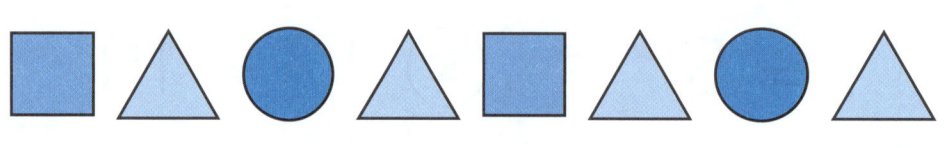
squares

4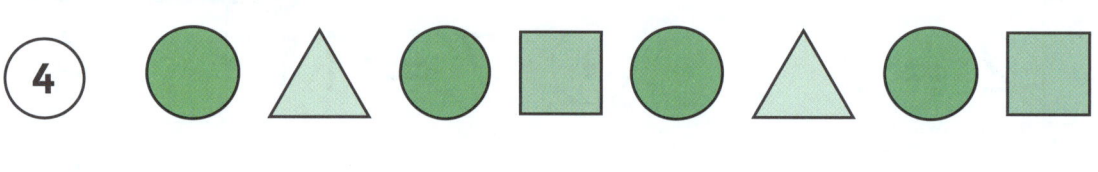
circles

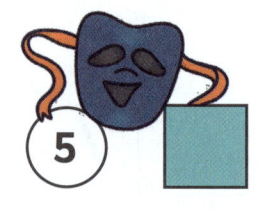 5
triangles

Today I scored  out of 5.

Week 11 — Day 5

Shade in the picture to show the right amount.   a half

1) a half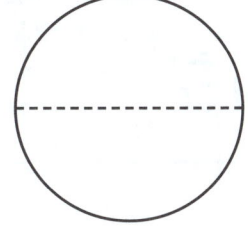

2) a quarter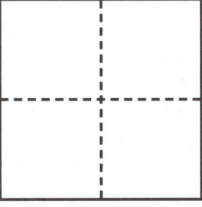

3) a quarter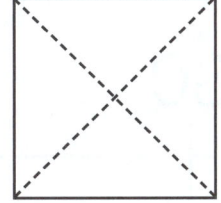

4) a half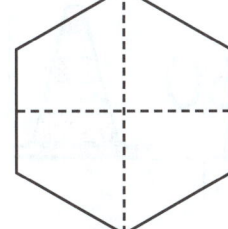

5) a quarter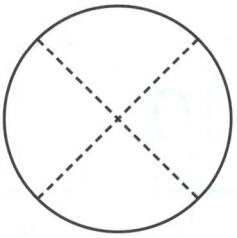

6) a half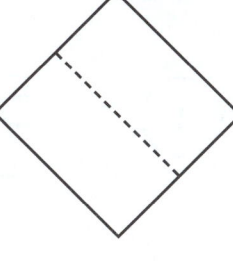

7) a half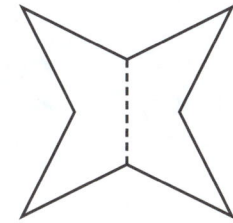

8) a quarter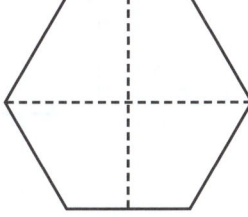

9) a half

10) a quarter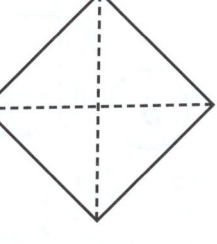

Today I scored ☐ out of 10.

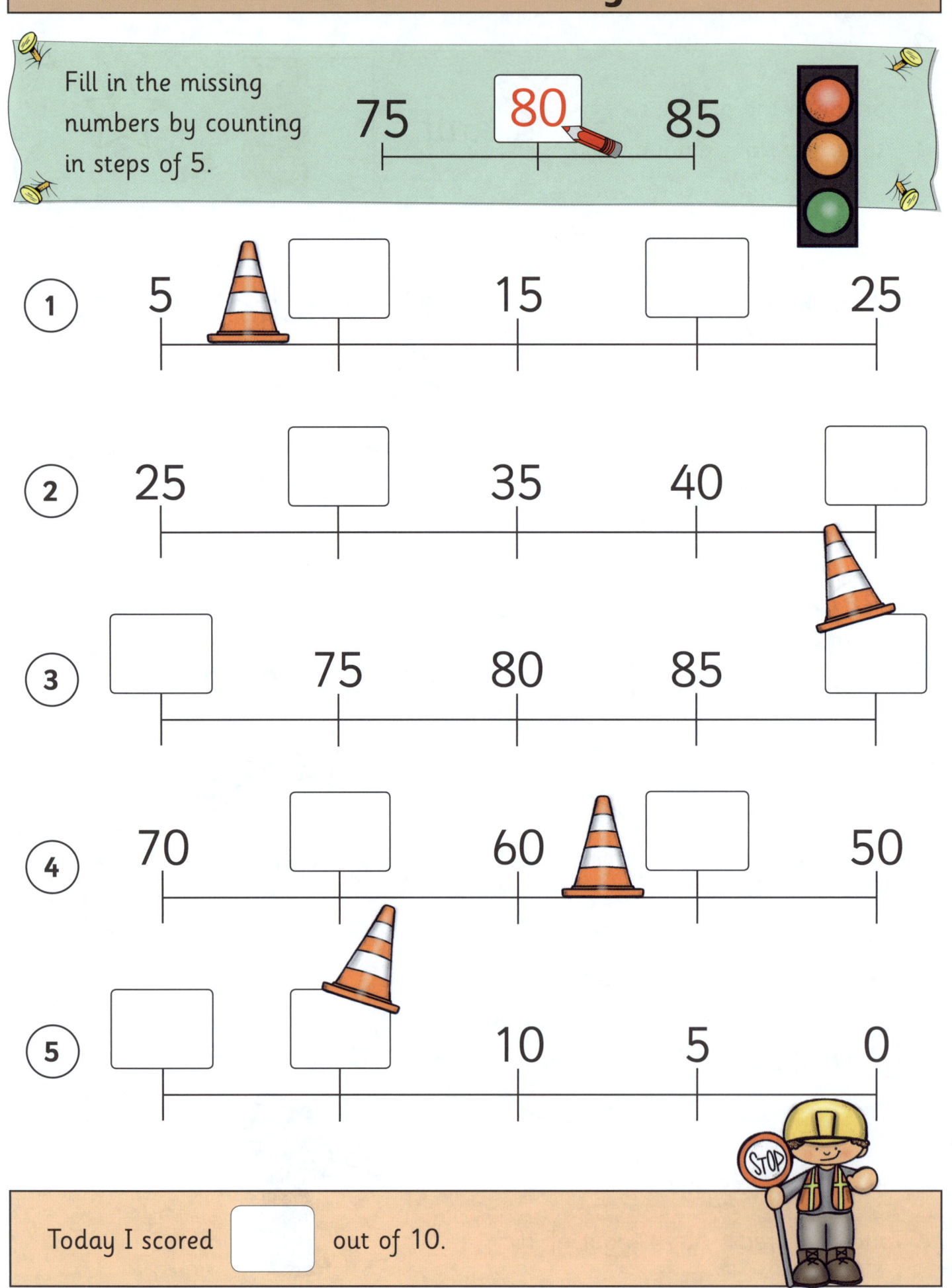

Week 12 — Day 2

Fill in the missing numbers.

13 + 2 = 15

1) 5 + 0 = ☐

2) 7 + 3 = ☐

3) 8 + 5 = ☐

4) 14 + 6 = ☐

5) 8 + ☐ = 10

6) 12 + 7 = ☐

7) 11 + ☐ = 20

8) ☐ + 9 = 9

9) 7 + ☐ = 16

10) ☐ + 9 = 15

Today I scored ☐ out of 10.

Week 12 — Day 4

Draw the new position of the spinner.

One quarter turn anticlockwise.

1. One half turn anticlockwise.

4. One whole turn anticlockwise.

2. Three quarter turns clockwise.

5. One half turn clockwise.

3. One quarter turn clockwise.

6. Three quarter turns anticlockwise.

Today I scored 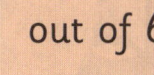 out of 6.

Week 12 — Day 5

Share the bones equally between the dogs by circling each group.

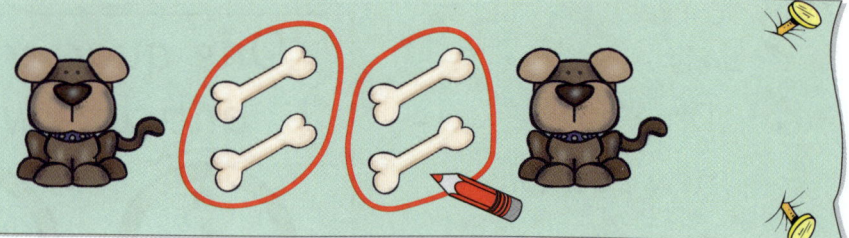

Today I scored ☐ out of 6.